This book is a work of fiction. It is based on a true story. Any similarities to actual events are coincidental. Copyright 2014 by Kip Stitts. No part of this book may be reproduced, stored in retrieval system or transmitted by any means, electronic or mechanical, without permission from the author.

ISBN-13 978-1505689730

ISBN 10- 1505689732

Dedication

To the creator, God for helping me through my journey. To my mother, Evelyn Stitts who is the greatest inspirational Queen that still lives inside of me. To my father, James Mallett for being there for me and moms. I will always love and appreciate you. To John Garth who was my mother's good friend. My brother who drove my mother many miles just to see her son. To attorney Sam Gun who suggested that I create this book. To Mr. Arthur Smith, thanks for being a wonderful friend. To Thomas A. Bruno, thanks for allowing me to know that I was not crazy, I was just going through a storm that you said I would come out of in the end. To Mary Oliver for the poem that I can identify with so well. Thank you very much. To Alberta Turner, a strong black Nubian queen. To my sisters and brothers and to my niece Latasha Stitts who always understands. To Patricia Patton a woman that was full of happiness. To Sonya Smith, the love of my life, the backbone of my storm, thanks and I will always love you. To my daughter Keirra Smith, the one who acts just like me, and to my daughter Kentoya Washington, my oldest with love. To my son Kip Michael Smith, the son that was sent from the most high. Thank you. To Sandra Washington: a mother that is always on the go, always helping people and always gives me her shoulder to lean on. Thank you for your support through my greatest storm. To Matthew M. Chambliss of Max Multi Media. Thank you for everything and for introducing me to Julius Justice who helped edit this book. To Jonathon Marshall and Robert Turner, the two most real friends I ever had in my life. Thanks very much for being a part of my life. Thanks very much for being a part of my life. To Orande Hall and Melvin Anderson, good friends that I have had in my life. To Marcellus Stitts, the nephew who always came to visit and buy his uncle a pack of cigarettes or a pop and would simply ask, Unc do you need anything during my storm. I love you for that, thank's for being a part of my life. A special shout out to all the nieces and nephews, aunties and cousins that played roles in my life. To Mark Naggy and Jonathon Marshall, again, the two most inspirational people in my life. Thanks for introducing me to real estate. To all the workers that ever worked for Kip. Kip appreciated the dedication, and hard work that each and every one of you put out. And last but not least, a shout out to all my extended family who I call my nieces and nephews.

And finally, to the people in my life who have used the game of power to manipulate, torment and torture me over the years. I bear you no grudges and I thank you very much. If I forgot to mention anyone, it was not intentional. Thank you, too.

Chapter 1

It was September, the year was 1999 and I had just been released from prison. I had been away from my family, friends and these streets for 10 long years. My Mom, who is and has always been my backbone, passed away one year prior to my release. I was blessed to be able to spend her last year with her because she would come to visit me every week before she died. I don't know what I would've done had I not had the opportunity to spend that time with her.

Once I was released on parole, I went to stay with my sister Betty. Upon my arrival everyone was very happy to see me and of course I was just as happy to be home. But, while everybody was happy and having a good time, I had only one thing on my mind and that was to get back to what I knew best: making money. My mother raised us to be family oriented. So, with that in mind, I wanted to make sure I included some of my family in my endeavors, so while still on parole I began to put things into play. Keep in mind, I had not been in a relationship in 10 long years so I pretty much didn't even know what that word meant. Back then, when I was with my daughter's mother, I thought I knew.

My new life all started when I met this girly named Pat (Patricia Patton). She was fine as hell; high yellow, about 5'11" with a great personality. When I first laid eyes on her I knew that I had to have her. She and my neighbor, Delrita were walking down Young Street when I spotted her. It was a known fact that Delrita smoked crack cocaine, and I would later find out that Pat

did as well. To get in good with
them, I told them that I had just
opened a spot over on Linnhurst &
Queen and that I had boulders
bigger than your shoulder. I knew
this would get Delrita to the spot
and since Pat was her friend, I
figured she'd come as well. At this
time I didn't know Pat was smoking
because she was thick and like I
said, fine as hell. So even before I
had all my information, I knew I
had to have her on my team. As it
turned out, once I got them over to
the spot, that would be all she wrote
for Pat. I couldn't pry her away
from that spot for nothing in the
world.

Pat had been at the spot for
about two or three days before I
knew she had a boyfriend. His name
was Tyrone. Tyrone had a
reputation for being tough. He also
had a reputation for locking women

up in houses and beating them. Pat was his latest victim. See everybody thought Tyrone was crazy because he was the bully of the neighborhood. I didn't know Tyrone, I just wanted to make sure that Pat, who I later found out they called "Pretty Girl," was alright.

After about a week, I'd go over to the house and ask Pat if she was hungry or I would just go over there and we would talk. It was during one of these conversations that I learned that Pat had a son named Maurice and that she was trying to get away from that crazy nigga, Tyrone. Once I heard that, I put her up under my wings and moved her into my sister's house without even first asking my sister. I didn't even know whether or not they would even get along, but I was on a mission.

Soon, Pat was working the spot for me with my nephew Keith. When I wasn't around, Keith ran the spot for me. After Pat moved in with my sister, she would go over to the spot every day and she and Keith would make money. After a while, the two of them became very close, like brother and sister. Of course, while all of this was going on Tyrone had been looking for her not knowing she was right there under his nose. Delrita told me "when he finds out where Pat is he's going to kick down your door." You see this is what he was known for doing around the hood. I told Delrita these exact words, "You got me fucked up!"

Anyway, one day while Pat was at the salon getting her hair and nails done, Tyrone found out where my spot was and came over, knocked on the door and asked for

Pat. Keith was there and he didn't know who Tyrone was, he thought he was a trusted friend, therefore, he told him that Pat would be back, she was at the hair salon. When Tyrone left, Keith called me and told me that he had come by looking for Pat. I asked him what he told him and he said, he told him where she was. "Awwwww shit," I responded. Then, me and my boy Bedrock headed over to the hair salon. Sure enough, as soon as we pulled up Tyrone was already there. When I saw him I immediately felt that I was going to have to kick his ass, but it turned out that I wouldn't have to. We talked for a minute and I told him that Pat was with me now. After I told him that, he asked Pat if that's what she wanted and she said yes. I was surprised, but after she said that he went on and left it alone. See Tyrone didn't know me anymore than I knew him,

11

but I'm sure he had heard about me and what I was about back in the day, so I guess that was enough for him to go on.

Chapter 2

Now that we were making a little money, Keith and Pat started spending a lot of time together; especially at the mall. They would spend their money on things like Guess jeans and all that other rich people shit. Me, I wasn't going to spend a dime because I had a place I would go and buy a pair of Lugz boots and two pair of pants and a shirt for $25.00 and I was good with that. The two of them would talk about me all the time, but I didn't care. They would tell me that I needed to come up to reality, but this was my reality.

After a while, I tried to help Pat get off drugs. I knew if she remained at the spot that it would be nearly impossible for her to kick the habit. So Keith and I urged her to leave and go get a job. Lucky for us she was willing to give it a shot, so she left and actually got a job. She was doing great for a few months and then she went missing. She was gone for about a week before she popped back up again. When I asked her where she was, she told me that she had been kidnapped, and I said, really, wow! But come to find out she had actually been around there with Tyrone locked up in the house smoking crack.

After that episode she came back home to me and I accepted her with open arms because by this time I had started falling in love with her. But Tyrone wasn't giving up lying down. The very next week while she was over on Cedar Grove visiting her girl Net, Tyrone caught up with her and took the car keys to my Cadillac which she was driving. Pat called me in a fit, so I flew around there without asking any questions. When I got over there, I smacked the shit out of Tyrone right in front of all his fans. After I did that, he made a motion like he was about to go for his gun, but before he could make another move I pulled mine out and told him, "Nigga, I told you to stop playing with me." After I took out my gun, everybody who was standing around started swinging on him, beating his ass. Yea, I know. Crazy right. From that day on as is often the case in the hood, Tyrone and I became good friends. It had even gotten to the point that if he ever saw Pat out on the streets doing something he knew I wouldn't agree with, he would tell her that he was going to tell me and he did.

Chapter 3

About two weeks after my confrontation with Tyrone, I moved out of my sister's house and rented a house on Joann Street. It would be Pat and I last house together. Although her son usually stayed with his grandmother, he moved in with us. I took him under my wings and treated him like my own. I helped him with his homework, took him to school and all that. This was the longest time Pat had taken care of Maurice. Her mother had kept him before hoping Pat would get herself together. When Ms. Patton met me, she knew I was the one for her daughter.

For Pat, dealing with me didn't come without its challenges because like her, I too had a past. Those challenges for her came with having to deal with my past relationships. I'd only had a few before I had gone to prison, but as a result of one of them I had a baby. She in particular was still in my life. Pat really liked her. Her name was Sonya. From observation, Pat could see where my heart was and that was with Sonya, who had been my first love. Pat was very smart; she was a long way from being stupid. She could tell that I was still very much in love with Sonya. When Pat was around or I was around Sonya, I tried to act like I didn't like Sonya because she had gotten married and had another child while I was in jail. But, Pat would test me. She would also use my relationship with Sonya as an excuse to run off and get high. She knew that Sonya and I were still having sex and whenever she thought we had been fucking, that's one of the excuses she would use to run off and get high.

Everybody loved Pat though, she was the type that would do anything for you. But like I said, she would try to test me in little ways to see if I loved Sonya more than her by saying petty little things like, "I bet Sonya won't make Maurice a sandwich." As she might if he were my biological son, but Sonya would turn around and do it for the love she had for me. Just little petty stuff like that. They both did things for the children because of their love for me. Pat would bend over backwards for my daughter.

Whenever Pat would run off and get high I would go out looking for her. I would find out where she was and end up having to kick down the door of some crack house because she had left me with her son for weeks. Be mindful, that I was getting money at this time, but also still dealing with her antics.

She would hide her car in some field and cover it with leaves and other debris so she could go missing. I would tell her time and time again, that one day I was going to leave her, because I was about to spread my wings (meaning I was about to get paid!). She would then get scared and act like she cared, but that crack had too much of a hold on her. She knew that I would do what I said because she was around all my old friends and they knew how things were for me before I went to jail. Her being out in the streets was dangerous, but my reputation and the fact that everybody liked her is what kept her safe.

Whenever my homeboy Tony would see her out somewhere all cracked out, he would call and tell me where she was. I'd then go to wherever she was and take the car without her even knowing. But, just like she was hooked on drugs….I was hooked on her. I loved the ground she walked on, but deep down inside, I knew that I was getting tired of playing her games. I wanted more out of life and spending my time trying to get her together was holding me up. So if that meant hooking up with someone else, that's what I would have to do. I knew I had to find that someone special.

Chapter 4

During this time, money was coming in good and I bought several cars. One was a new 2000 Cadillac truck, which I never really drove. It was the short body style, gold in color with tan interior. Betty drove it most of the time; I only drove it when I was going someplace special. Also during this time, I began to feel like my plan was coming together. I had a good connect and everything was working out well. My connect was located in Grand Rapids so me and my boy Bedrock drove up there about two to three times a week to do business. Our plug was cool, he used to come to the D all the time and he and Bedrock would hang out. We were pretty close, too. I just didn't hang out as much as them. I was more laid back and about my money. The connects name was Marlowe and we did good business together. Meaning I always kept the count right.

Pretty soon I got turned on to another hustle. That of buying, renting and selling houses. My homeboy Jay introduced me to one of his connections in real estate by the name of Mark Naggy. Mark taught me how to invest in houses and flip them. The first house I bought was located at 19928 McKay. After that I immediately bought homes on Jane and Carrie streets. The house on McKay was me and Bedrock's safe house, where we kept all of our supplies and money. We called it the Bat Cave. It was low key and sat way back from the street in a good neighborhood. No one knew about it but Marlowe, Bedrock and me. We made a pact that no one could know where the Bat Cave was but us.

By this time my patience with Pat was steadily growing short. I often shared my concerns with my boy Marlowe so he knew that I was in need of a good strong woman to help me get to the top. Little did I know he knew just the right person, she was a young lady he purchased clothes from. He would always talk about her, telling me how she was on top of her game and that I really needed to meet her cause she didn't have a man. He said together he could see us making a whole lot of money. My home boy WeWe (Perry) was dealing with her as well. I met WeWe while we were doing time together, he's a good guy. We did a little business together, but not too much. We were more friends than anything.

One day while WeWe and I were together, he said that he had to make a stop because he wanted to purchase a few things from this girl that sold clothes from her crib. He wanted to buy an Iceberg shirt and a coat, so I said "okay, let's go." So, we pulled up to an apartment over on Chene, got out and went in. When I stepped into the apartment I knew there was something special about this young lady, I mean she had clothes everywhere. Her name was Anita. She wasn't all that good looking to me at the time, she looked alright, but I was still impressed. The only thing going through my head at the time, was, "damn, is this the young lady that Marlowe was also talking about!" In my mind, I thought, yea o.k., this girl got game. I immediately felt like I needed her as a part of my team. She was the missing link. After a brief observation, I noticed she had the ability to think, the drive to go get, the determination to win and the motivation to achieve success by any means. That was my diagnosis of her, which to me, made us so compatible. She was the woman missing in my life and I was the man missing in hers.

Chapter 5

Other than a few of my boys, not too many people knew that I was getting money, because I wasn't the flashy type. I had a construction company called "Kip's Home Improvement" and I would never dress up and always drove an old station wagon, but I had a stash-spot hidden in it. A few people kinda knew I was getting money, but they didn't know to what capacity. Anyway, WeWe put in an order for a Pelle Pelle coat and a few other things because she was out of the coat that he wanted. He introduced me to Anita as Shorty Mac and I asked her did she get kids clothes and she said she did and asked what size I needed. I told her I didn't know and that my daughter was petite. Then I snuck in a play and asked her "if she had room in her life for a friend?" She said no, but I didn't blame her for her response because I was looking a mess. I looked more like I was working for WeWe, so in her mind I'm sure she thought I was a nobody, but in my mind I had to get her. She had her own apartment, a car, a job and she was hustling, so I got her number on the pretense of just staying in touch. I think even back then, I was underestimating her a little. Yeah, she was getting money and all that, but this girl really knew the streets and had been around the block a few times. I also later found out that she had been treated wrong by several men in the past, and didn't waste a lot of time letting me know that. When we got back to the car, I asked WeWe what was up with that and he said, she had recently gotten hustled out of $10,000 during a business trip, but he had showed her how to get the money back.

Anyway, I waited a couple of days to call about the coat and clothes for my daughter and we ended up talking for a few hours. I must say that I can have a sense of humor and a way of making people feel comfortable around me. While we were talking I took it upon myself to ask her again if I could take her out. She laughed and asked "When?" Wow! Just the response I was looking for. That was the happiest day of my life. After hearing that response I immediately went into action. We set the date up for the next day. Remember, I had been in jail during my 20's and hustling since I was 14, so I had never really played the dating game cause up until that time Sonya was my life. I had been with a couple of other girls; Fuzzy and Tama, but we were kids. I was a child when I left the streets and had returned home a grown man, but with mixed emotions.

The next day I went to pick up my truck from my sister, put on my best clothes and went to pick up Anita. My connect had put in a good word for me. He told Anita that I was a good guy and that she should give me a chance. When I arrived to pick her up you could tell she had never been with a gentleman because when I got out to open the door for her she ran to the passenger side and said she wasn't driving. I told her I was just walking around to open the door for her and she burst out laughing.

I really don't remember all the places we went that night, but I do remember going to the Outback Steakhouse and that's when I discovered how much that girl could eat. You know how people can be shy for the first time, well that wasn't her. She ordered a 17-20 ounce steak with a baked potato and an order of coconut shrimp and ate it like it was her last meal. But that was cool. We had a good time that night. She really enjoyed herself. From that day on I really enjoyed being around her. I was impressed. That first night I spent the night with her, but again I was a gentleman and didn't try anything. We even slept in the same bed. I didn't try to have sex with her because I knew she was the one for me.

Chapter 6

After that night, I left the house that I was sharing with Pat and moved by myself into the Bat Cave over on McKay. Although I left Pat, I didn't leave her life completely. I was trying to find happiness, while allowing her to find happiness as well.

Not long after I left she met this guy name Mark and started dating him. I loved Pat and just wanted her to get herself together. On occasion, I would help her and Mark out financially. I didn't mind because I knew this made things easier for her.

Anita and I didn't jump right into a relationship though, we waited about a month before we actually had sex. For whatever reason, I could tell that Anita didn't have a lot of experience in that field, but nevertheless, after we made love I was all in. Not so much because of the sex, but what I thought I could make our sex life become. I even took her to the Bat Cave. This was how I really got her because up until that point she thought I was just a nobody. That is until she saw all the money on the floor that Bedrock was counting. I only took her there to impress her, but when I saw Bedrock's face when we walked in, I knew I had fucked up because of the pact. I cared, but I cared about her more. I also couldn't really blame him for being upset, but I had to show this girl who she was dealing with. Don't get me wrong, Bedrock and I was cool. We had met in jail and had hit it off immediately from day one. He was just real and down to earth. The thing that I liked about him was he wasn't a fighter or hard hustler he was just cool. Anyway my plan worked. After that day, Anita was all in.

When I introduced her to my family and my team, everybody liked her except Betty and Bedrock. Betty said she could see right straight through her and so did Bedrock. They both told me that she was not right for me, but hard-headed me didn't want to hear any of it, I was doing my thing. After the month I waited to have sex, Anita and I became the best of friends.

In my eyes, Anita didn't like to have sex, and like I said nor did she have any experience at it, but I didn't care, I just wanted to have her in my life and a part of my team. She even thought I was helping her sell all her clothes, but I wasn't. I sold some of the items, but the rest I was just giving away to friends and the team.

Not long after this, I got my truck back from my sister and gave it to Anita to drive and she had it from then on. I was so excited, I couldn't wait to introduce her to my boy Jay, who was one of my best friends, because it had gotten that serious. I also introduced her to other members of my team, like, Mr. Will X, Pat, Keith, Tim and Lucky, my man from jail. When Lucky got out, I put him on and we were getting money for real. We were doing anywhere from 50 to 100 deals a week

Chapter 7

Before long, Anita and I moved in together. We got a nice place downtown at the Riverfront Apartments. There were a few things I had to get used to but nothing serious. For example, I knew that Anita dealt with a lot of men because she sold clothes, so I wasn't jealous when they would come around; I allowed her to do her thing. Bedrock on the other hand was mad as hell with me for centering my life around her. When she would get off work I was there, when she called I was there, it became all about Anita. I would stop working after 4:30 p.m. so I could beat her home.

Along the way there were little things that I began to find out about her. One of them being that she was a big show off. She liked to hang out and do it up big. She reminded me of my boy Lucky, that's my man. He liked to do it big, too. Fake it till you make it was their motto. We got money and Lucky and Anita hit it off the very first time they met because they were just alike. I didn't do it big like them, but I spoiled her rotten. I bought her everything; furs....coats, gold, diamonds, whatever her heart desired.

See Lucky knew that I was a laid back type of guy getting lots of money. Anita also knew, but she didn't act like it. What I mean by that is for example, her favorite clubs were Floods as well as the River Rock. Floods is located across the street from Greektown Casino and The River Rock was located downtown right off the river. It was a place where all the ballers and gangsters liked to flash their success. I tried to get her out of there by telling her those niggas would kidnap her, duct tape her and dump her ass in a trunk just to get money from me. You would have thought she would've cared, but she didn't because she was in her 20's and feeling really good about herself and why not, she was young, with a Boss ass nigga who had a Cadillac truck, two Benzes, a Corvette and lots of money. She was on top of the world and she wasn't about to let nothing or nobody take that away from her.

I would later find out the hard way about Anita's true personality. And it wasn't pretty.

Looking back, if I knew what I know now, I would have kept it strictly business during that time, but I allowed her to know what I was doing and made my life around hers.

Anita had a lot of female friends. They called themselves the Single Mingle Crew. She had this one friend named Yolanda who worked for Johnson Controls. Yolanda was fine and she carried herself like a true lady at all times. She was about 5' 7" tall, thick as hell, brown skinned and she was single. I remember one day we went to a skating party and Anita invited Yolanda. Anita told her that me and a couple of my boys would be there so she would have a nice time because that's how we do. The moment Lucky saw Yolanda he knew he had to have her, Anita also put a good word in for him. She told her that Lucky was driving a DTS Deville which was parked right in front of the door and that Lucky was balling hard.

Throughout this entire time, Betty and Bedrock kept telling me that Anita wasn't shit (that she was a rat), but I still wasn't hearing it. I loved her and her family, we all got along great. Her mother and father were deaf, but they both knew how to sign really well. I wrote notes to her mother and her mother loved me like a son. Anita's sister Jess was my girl. We even paid her way through college. I also paid Anita's way through school and would help her with her homework. She obtained a Master's Degree in Business Management. While I was paying their way I should've been getting my own degree.

Her family structure was different from mine. These people loved school and were very smart, with the exception of Jazz. Jazz was the black sheep of the Power family, but just like my family, I treated them like my own. I even got their moms house out of foreclosure for $28,000, at least that's what Anita said she needed the money for. She knew she had my heart.

See Anita was the head of the family; they all looked up to her. She was the oldest amongst Jess, Ann and Jazz. They also have three other sisters on their father's side who are all older than Anita; they were cool too and liked me as well.

One day me and Anita were having this conversation about buying this restaurant and I was all for it until she mentioned this dude named Lamar. Lamar used to sell clothes for Anita and was one of those smooth talkers, always trying to come up on whomever. I still don't know to this day what other type of relationship they had because he was a fake it till he make it type of nigga.

Anyway, the building was on Kelly Rd. and Lamar knew this guy who would lease us the building with some of the equipment, but not all of it. They put the deal together for the restaurant with the man I later came to know as Bruce and he, Anita and Lamar signed the lease; nowhere did it say Anita and Kip or just Anita. When I asked her about it she replied, "Because Bruce wouldn't let her get it without Lamar's name on the lease because Lamar was his boy and he was doing it for him."

Ok, I went for that bullshit line.

I told Anita that if the restaurant was what she wanted then that was fine with me.

The building was a mess inside and out. It needed some major cash to get it up and running so we had to hire a construction company to do the work. Thank God Kip's Home Improvement would be able to do it all. Man, it took about $40,000 to get the inside and outside ready. My team and I put it together in about two weeks. We made the place look like a new building. The sign on the top of the building read: Love's Fish and Shrimp.

We were all so proud. Don't forget I still didn't know Lamar's last name, I was just happy to be a part of this with my girl Anita. Plus, I figured it would keep her out of my business in the streets. Bedrock was also happy about the place because he could see us being out the streets one day. He didn't mind dealing with Anita on this tip, but he still didn't like her. Nevertheless, we were off and running.

Me, Anita, Lamar, and Bedrock all cooked at the restaurant. Man, we were doing good. I don't even know till this day how much the lease was every month, but we were making money. At least seven hundred to a thousand dollars a day and that is from the day we opened until the day we closed. The food was good and easy to cook. It was all about the batter.

Lucky would bring his people to the restaurant all the time to get food.

After a while Lamar began to see what I was about and realized that he needed to get on my team, but I wouldn't put him on because I didn't trust him.

Eventually me and Bedrock had to get back to the streets so to replace us in the kitchen; Anita had to hire some more people because me and Bedrock couldn't be there like that. So she hired a couple of her cousins. She even hired her sister Toni on her father's side, to come and help out. She also hired a couple other people to help out. One of them was a lady named Carol. Carol also did our taxes as well as everybody else's taxes and was good at getting people money back.

We did what we had to do at the restaurant to make it work, including hiring and firing. It was strictly business; if they didn't do right they had to go. Carol did right all the time, but Anita would give her hell and wonder why she would come in late and not do anything to Anita's satisfaction. The only time Anita would be nice to her was when she wanted her to do taxes or something of that nature. Carol was very good in the beginning, but you see Anita wasn't too good of a people person...she didn't know how to talk to people. The only thing on her mind was money and she was very controlling. but she knew how to make that money. Therefore, her mother and father as well as her sisters were very proud of us.

From day one, I never trusted Lamar with his smooth talking ass. When Toni came around, he acted like he liked her, and was trying to get with her, but I wasn't sure if he was playing a role just trying to throw me off because he and Anita really had something going on between them.

Chapter 8

When it came to a lot of things Anita didn't like to listen. You see she thought she knew it all because she was going to school and had it together, at least in her mind you couldn't tell her nothing. Yes, she was selling clothes, but that little money was barely enough for her to pay her rent, car note and attend school even though she was working. What Anita didn't realize at the time was that she had a man that would be there for her through the good and the bad. But she didn't realize that. I guess she thought I was the type of guy who would fuck over her, like a few of the men she had dated in the past.

My plan was for her to finish school and we'd open a bunch of businesses so that I could clean up all the money I had in the streets and get out of the game and eventually that did happen.

Turns out she just wanted to fuck over me because she never had anyone in her life like Kip. Whatever type of person she was when she was with other people, I don't know. I'm sure people must have fucked over her because she sure was beginning to give me hell. I wasn't just in love with her. I loved her like a sister. She was my best friend and I trusted her with my life.

I really don't know how it came out, but one day I received the shock of my life. Me, Lucky, Bedrock and Lamar were talking and the name Love came up and for some reason I asked Lamar what his last name was and he said Love. I was floored! I couldn't believe what I was hearing. Love's was the name of the restaurant. I was embarrassed and mad at the same time. So I said you telling me your name is Lamar Love and he replied yes. I immediately jumped up and called Anita. I told her that I needed to talk to her and to come down to the restaurant.

When she got there, I asked Anita why in the hell wouldn't she tell me that she named this restaurant after Lamar, but before she could respond I went crazy. I started throwing furniture and flipping shit…I became a mad man. It got so bad that she ended up calling the police. When they arrived she told them what happened and they put me off the property because my name wasn't on the lease. I told the police that this was our place together, but she told them something else, which only made me angrier. She told them something like her and Lamar were partners and that I was not an owner, which got me to thinking that they were fucking and had played me the entire time. I couldn't think straight after that.

I laid low and waited until closing time and watched her pull off. She was in the black Benz I had bought and I was in my truck. After she pulled off and had driven a little ways, I pulled up behind her doing about 90 and rammed my truck dead into the back of that car...I didn't give a fuck! At first we were headed straight in the direction of the motorcycle shop on Houston Whittier at the end of Gratiot and I was just about to ram her through the shop when she turned left and headed for the police station. But I didn't care; I was going to push her ass through the front entrance of the police station even if it meant destroying the entire building. The only thing I knew was that this bitch had played me and she was going to pay.

Before I could carry out my plan though the police was on my ass 10 cars deep. Again, I didn't care. I was going to kill this bitch. They eventually blocked us off and surrounded my truck with their guns drawn and ordered me to get out of the truck and on the ground. One of the officers knew what I was going through, because I had talked to him at the restaurant and explained to him the situation. But I still l had to leave because my name was not on the lease. Anyhow, because of this knowledge, he didn't allow the other officers to treat me badly.

I was cuffed and taken into the 9th Precinct and charged with malicious destruction of personal property. I received 5 years' probation as a result of that charge. From this alone, this should have been the first and last time that I fucked with Anita Power.

Chapter 9

After I got out of jail, I went home to 19928 McKay. I was hurt and disappointed, but I was making it. Pat would come over to check on me and try to get back with me, but I didn't want to be with Pat anymore like that. She was my dog, my friend and I did everything in my power not to allow her to take advantage of me, I was vulnerable because I was emotionally fucked up. Unfortunately on this one particular day, my penis wasn't hearing it and before long we were making love. I tried to push her away, but she leaned over and unzipped my pants, took out my dick and started licking and kissing all over it. After that it was all over. I was all in. After we finished making love, I thanked her but I still tried to convince her to go back with Mark because he was a nice guy. Although I later found out that he was a mess, but at the time I had a lot of respect for him because he had accepted her and her son as one. But Pat fucked that up with him when she got caught with the white boy Don. You see, Pat had built Mark up, and taught him everything I had taught her about real estate and rehabbing houses, but in the end, he would run off and leave her hanging.

After a month or so, Anita got back to calling me and hanging up the phone when I answered. This went on for a while, her constantly calling and hanging up. One day she had one of her sister's call to butter me up. I guess it worked because I started dropping my guards. Her sister wasn't mad at me and understood where I was coming from. All I really remember is that she asked me not to hurt Anita. She said that if we couldn't get along that I should just take the loss and keep it moving.

I should've taken her advice.

Next, Anita's mom started texting me all the time. She even stopped by to see me. Meanwhile, Anita was still playing on the phone. One day I picked it up and it was her sister Jazz. The two of them were at the shop together. Me and Jazz exchanged pleasantries, but the thing is I guess Anita was missing me because she had two of her sister's and her momma calling me. She was trying to find out how to get back in my good grace. I guess she realized that she hadn't robbed me for enough, so she was coming back for more.

As all of this was going on, Bedrock was happy as hell it was over. He reminded me that he had told me she wasn't right for me. He told me I had brought her to the bat cave where we agreed no one was supposed to know about. But I still didn't listen to him; little did he know I had allowed her family to talk me into talking back with Anita.

One day Jazz put her on the phone and that was all she wrote. We ended up talking for hours.

Remember, Anita didn't like having sex. So of course oral sex was out of the question. But she called with that sweet talk saying, "Kip, I love you and I'm sorry if I hurt you and I'm going to put Lamar out today and we can stay in business." I said okay, but I told her I wanted her to change the name and she agreed. She then closed down the shop and came right over. Man, she didn't even know how to have sex, but she tried her little heart out that night. We did it all night long; I guess she thought she put it on me. Yeah, right. It was never about the sex with me, it was always about her mind. That's what I was in love with.

Chapter 10

This time, I didn't move in with her, but I knew I couldn't stay at the bat cave because I kept running in and out and I knew that was drawing too much attention.

True to her word, Anita did exactly what she said she was going to do, she put Lamar out and changed the name of the restaurant from Love's Fish and Shrimp to Good Fish and Shrimp and she and I were back in business. We ran the restaurant for about three months before we ran into trouble. Someone came in and robbed the customers. Anita was not robbed because she was behind the bullet proof glass. But there were about 8 to 10 people in the restaurant at the time and they were robbed. I wasn't there, but it was a mess....

About a month after that, they caught me and her after closing up shop and robbed us again. I could tell the guy was an amateur because the nigga barely knew what he was doing. Anita was already in the truck so I told her to pull off because he only had a 22 pistol to my head. Calling her a bitch, he yelled that if she pulled off that he would kill me, so she gave him the money. He then told me to give him my money, so I gave the nigga a hundred dollars along with my I.D. which was also in my pocket. The hundred dollars is all I generally kept in one pocket. I knew he would think that was all I had cause that's how people think, but I had about $4,000 in my other pocket. He then demanded my coat, so I handed it to him and he left, but not before tossing my I.D. on the ground. I guess he wasn't trying to take it there. After he left, I got into the truck with Anita and called my boys and we looked for that nigga all night.

It seemed like it was beginning to be one thing after the other. After getting robbed, the restaurant caught fire and burned down a month later. We had insurance, but the owner of the building Bruce didn't, and wanted Anita to give him some of our insurance money. Real shit. I didn't even know how much we got back from the insurance company, but at the time I didn't care. As long as we got back what I had put into it I was satisfied. I was getting money, but I also wasn't trying to just throw money away. Still Anita was pocketing it all.

After the insurance situation I went back to the streets full time. One of the guys that I fronted supplies to named Dru, introduced me to his side chick named Barbara. The guy was a mess, but he didn't jerk over my money. Dru always called me big bro and every time Dru took Barbara through something, she would call me. I would talk to her for a while and tell her that I was going to get him together. Mainly because she was the one holding all of the supplies and money I had fronted him.

Meanwhile, I had been dealing with my man Mark Naggy at this point for about two years or so, rehabbing some of his properties. Anita and I came up with the idea that we should go into real estate together, since I had already been in the business and had the connections, so we opened A&K Investments and got an office located downtown in the Penobscot Building. We started off finding investors to buy the homes we were fixing up for Mark. Eventually we branched off on our own. I remember our first investor, it was this guy named Mark Johnson and his wife.

Mark Johnson was a good friend of mine, we had attended school together. He also had a child by my twin sister Kim. We did about three or four deals with Mark. He made about $7,000 off each deal. The first house we bought was on McKay in the 1700 block. After that there was no looking back. We were off and running. We got a good deal on the McKay property. We got it for the price of a two bedroom but it was a 3 bedroom that we purchased for $18,000. We only had to invest about $6,000 to bring it up to par and that took the total investment up to $24,000. We gave the investor

$7,000 off the property so that took us up to $29,000. We ended up selling the property for about $78,000. Therefore we made a profit of $39,000 after closing cost. We was killing 'em.

By this time I was ready to move into a place off the river because Anita and I still weren't trying to live together, although we were doing everything else together. So I moved down to the River Place Apartments. I used my sister Betty and Anita's dad to co-sign the lease for me, that's how I got it. Man, the apartment was out cold. It was on the top floor. My rent was $2,200 a month. When you first walked in, you walked through the foyer, and then there was a long hallway about 10 feet wide and 50 feet long which led to some double doors which led you into the apartment. When you opened the double doors there was a big open space with a living room, dining room and a nice modern stainless steel kitchen off to the side. There was also a staircase in the living room which led to an upstairs bathroom, the bedrooms, as well as a walkway that overlooked the lower living area.

All it needed was my taste of furniture. I wondered how I would decorate it, but I knew whatever I came up with, I would lay it out. I loved it.

Chapter 11

Mark Naggy loved doing business with us because we did good business. But, for the time being I was intent on staying in the street. Anita had other ideas though. She told all my boys she was going to get me off the streets because we had found our field. I allowed the boys to know that when and if I did get off the streets, they could follow and that I would have roles for everybody.

During this time there was a whole lot going down. Anita and I became good business partners. For me, our relationship as lovers was no longer a priority. We were living in different homes and we were riding and living very good.

Meanwhile, my little man Dru was trying to find somewhere else for Barbara to live. Why I didn't know. We moved her into a two family flat on Jane Street to an upstairs flat and used the downstairs as a meeting place for the crew. Like I said before, Dru was a mess. He blew money, fucked up cars and just wouldn't listen.

During this time Pat and Bedrock had become very close and Anita had become close to the both of them. This didn't matter at first, but as time would pass their relationship would turn out bad for me because Anita now knew my every move. And believe me, they told it all.

When you're doing business, in the beginning you make a lot of mistakes and we made our share. In the early years, the mistake that hurt the most was when Anita put all of our eggs in one basket. She had all of our money tied up for about 60 days. We owed Home Depot about $15,000 or $20,000, we owed car notes and insurance on three cars, we owed rent on both apartments and we owed American Express and numerous other creditors. While all this was going on, Anita decided to run off to her mother's house and stay knowing we owed all these people. We weren't broke; there was just a hold up on our money for a while. She didn't tell me what was going on until everything had gotten out of control.

Back then we were not organized at all. She was doing the best she could running her side of the business and I was doing the best I could. My friends, family and myself were working on these houses at low pay at first trying to make it happen and I was using all the street money to put the houses together. After Anita finally told me what was going on with us financially, I went and paid Home Depot and gave her the money to pay off everything else. After that we had made all the mistakes we were going to make.

So now it was time to move on. We got a bigger space in the Penobscot Building and opened up First Equity Investments Corp.

At this time we didn't know a lot about the schemes that were out there and how to run a corporation or how people would try and trick us out of our money, but we would soon find out. We had put it all out there on the line.

This was how it was supposed to work. We would find investors with a 650 or better credit score to purchase 3 to 5 houses from us. We would give them $5,000 off each property. Then we would rehab the property and put in all new appliances, etc. Once everything was completed, we would put a Section 8 tenant into the property, plus put insurance on the property for a year.

Our profit was supposed to be $10,000 off each property, but I knew we were making more than that. I didn't care because Anita had our back and I knew she would make sure our money was good. To help make sure we stayed on top of things we also hired a secretary, her name was Shantia. We also hired a Section 8 coordinator named Bedillia. With them in place and Anita in charge, our paperwork was very organized.

While Anita was in charge of all the paperwork and the investors, I dealt with all the contractors and did all the street running to make sure the properties were completed on time. After getting an assignment, each contractor had 30 days to complete a house, no matter how much damage there was. In the early days, we started off slow, but soon we were doing about 30 houses a month with 28 contractors. We were feeding a lot of families. However, life couldn't be good enough for Anita and she went to fucking over people.

Anita was good at manipulating people and getting them to believe what she wanted them to believe. I'm shaking my head now, because we had such a great business going.

Chapter 12

When my man Dru went to jail, some kind of way, me and his girl Barbara started kickin' it. Remember that me and Anita's sex life was not well at all. Anyway, one day I went over to Jane Street to collect the rent money from Barbara. When I got there she told me she'd had a dream about me. I didn't know that she liked me because she would often call me and tell me about what Dru did and I would tell her it was going to be alright, not knowing that one day I would be in bed with her. I was supposed to be helping her deal with whatever problems she was going through.

The night we had sex, I was trying to help them. I just wanted to help fulfill her dream as a friend for just one night, however, things didn't work out that way. That night I left, went and did what I had to do business wise, but was back at her house within a few hours. Why did I do that? When I arrived at her place she had set the mood for romance. She had placed rose petals from the bottom of the stairs to the top. When I entered into the apartment, seeing the rose petals threw me off and my heart skipped a beat. When I saw her, she was looking sexy as hell standing in front of me in this beautiful two piece purple lingerie and was wearing some six inch heels to boot. I could barely speak. In a slight whisper, I told her how sexy she looked. By now I was hooked. There were flowers throughout the room, and sexual healing by Marvin Gaye was playing in the background. Located on the table was a bottle of champagne sitting on ice with two glasses ready with candles on each side of the glasses. She took me by the hand, picked up the glasses and led me to the bedroom. When we got upstairs, the bedroom was decorated with mirrors on the ceiling as well as the walls. She placed her hands on my shirt and began to unbutton it and then did the same with my pants. After I was naked she led me into the bathroom where a hot bubble bath awaited us. As I placed one foot into the tub, she leaned over and kissed me and my dick responded accordingly. She was also hot. But I was patient. I wanted to savor every moment and so did she. After we finished our passionate, fun filled bubble bath, she led me back into the bedroom where we made the best love of our lives. From that point on, I was hooked!

The problem is that and I'll admit it; I'm a stone freak and Barbara was there to satisfy my every need. Barbara and I were sexually amazing together. From that first day on, she became my Lil' Mama. Every free chance I got, I was with her having hot passionate sex. And every day I wasn't with her, I was thinking about her.

Of course, once my other lady friends found out about her I was in trouble. Pat was the first to find out. She really didn't like the fact that I was about to put this bitch on my team. You see, I guess I have a way of creating monsters because if you're in my circle my philosophy is; whatever's mine is yours. Pat knew this because of the way I treated her and I still had her back. Bedrock was cool, but he didn't like the fact that I was about to put

Barbara on the team either. He knew that Barbara was Dru's girl and that could create a problem. Little did he know that Dru didn't give a fuck about Barbara. Deep down I knew it wasn't my business to mess with her, but the sex made me not care.

That was my baby, she was a soldier and I needed her in my life. She made me feel like a king. She cooked for me and brought my food to me on a platter in bed. She picked up after me. She really knew how to treat a man. Anita didn't do any of that, but I still loved Anita and wasn't about to leave her for Barbara. No, Barbara didn't have nothing when I met her, but nor did anyone else. They just didn't want her to get a piece of the pie.

Pat had a man, but I was still taking care of her and her son, so she shouldn't of had anything to say about my Lil' Mama. But, she was so mad and jealous that she went and told Anita everything she knew about Barbara.

After she did that, my life began and ended at the same time.

Anita started to investigate and question Bedrock, Lucky and all my team about me. During this time I had introduced Barbara to my family. Of course they liked her. She was the coolest. She was very understanding. She knew that I had a woman and she knew how to play her role.

I cared so much for Barbara that I bought her a car; a 1989 Taurus. Man, turns out that would become one of the best investments I've ever made. The car was right on time. The day after I bought it, me and Bedrock had to go do a deal with this guy named Jim. I had met Jim through a mutual friend by the name of James, who was finding properties for me and Anita. His brother Jason and his Dad had a collision shop on Gratiot and I used to refer a lot of business their way.

Anyway, he knew I was in the streets as well as into real estate. Plus, Jim also sold cars and I had done some business with him on that tip also, so he wanted me to meet his brother who worked at Jack Christian's Realty. Come to find out, Jim was an informant. I found out after we met at his office in Southfield. When I got there, we talked for a while after which I gave him money for a package. I usually didn't do business like that or give anyone my money, but this was my man James and Jason's people. I let Jim know that I was laid back and didn't deal with a lot of people. He said okay and that he would call me later and have me to pick up my package. When the call came in I was with my Lil' Mama and her son Bee. Jim told me to meet him at the Burger King on Evergreen. I didn't know too much about the west side, I was just learning it because of the real estate game. It was about 7:30 or 8:30 p.m. when he called asking me what I was driving, but I didn't tell him. I told Bedrock that he didn't have to go and that I was going to take care of it. So I took Lil' Mama instead and drove her car.

When we arrived at the location, he wasn't there and I had to keep calling him because every time I called he would tell me he was on his way. While waiting, I started getting this strange feeling so I started looking around. Sure enough as I started surveying the area, I realized that the only cars in the area appeared to be unmarked police cars. But, I was intent on taking care of my business so I remained calm. When he called back the last time he said that his people were pulling up and I told him that I didn't want to meet anybody else. He said he had gotten caught up and his people were gonna place the bag in a certain garbage container. Well these fools pulled up alright. They pulled up with music blasting like straight young thugs. They tossed the bag in the can and pulled off. I waited a minute or so then pulled up to the can and told Lil Mama to get the bag. Keep in mind I was still looking at what I believed to be unmarked police cars, but I wasn't sure if I was just tripping or what. I hoped I was.

When Lil' Mama retrieved the bag, I looked into it, and there was nowhere near what I had ordered. So I called Jim as I was driving off, but he didn't answer. I then looked into my rearview mirror to see what I was now sure were the police following me. One car pulled up beside me and motioned for me to pull over! I looked at my Lil' Mama and told her I wasn't going back to jail and smashed down on the accelerator!

I took off flying down the street going nowhere fast because I didn't know the area. About seven police cars were chasing me. The car I had just bought opened up like it had a 454 up under the hood. I got to a block where some guys were hanging and threw the shit out the window then rode about a mile down and jumped out the car. I ran into a wooded area lost as hell. I didn't know where I was. I stopped and hid my money under this big brick then found a place and ducked down hoping the police wouldn't see me. I had left my Lil' Mama and her son in the car. When I hopped out the car she was a trooper, she told me to "Go Big Daddy" and I went. When the police pulled up on her and her son they asked her where the fuck I went and she told them she didn't know, that I had just jumped out and ran.

While one group of cops was out looking for me, a few others stayed back to interrogate her. They asked her what my name was and she said she didn't know me. She said she had just met me a few days prior at Belle Isle and we had hooked up to go eat.

I was worried about my Lil' Mama because I didn't know what

she was going to say about me, but she held her own. That got me to really loving her even more. But, I couldn't allow her to know that I was deeply in love with her like that.

Well, I didn't know the area well, but the police obviously did. They found me hiding in the bush, handcuffed me and took me in. They also found the money, about $2,300.

Turns out they couldn't hold me because they didn't find the stuff that I had tossed out the window. They held me for about two or three hours then let me out the back door. Thank God!

As soon as I got out I called Bedrock and told him that Jim had set me up and that I was on my way back to Jane in a cab. Lil' Mama was happy to know that I was out so she could let me know someone had broken in down stairs. She said she saw a white Tahoe truck that looked like Lucky's. But they didn't find anything in the house. But wow, I wondered if Lucky would even try something like that after all I had done for him. Anita never knew what was going on cause I tried to keep her out of the streets and staying focused on the business.

The next day me and Bedrock went to Jim's office like gangsters and told him to give us our money back. Of course he was surprised to see us because he thought we were locked up. He nervously went into a drawer and gave me the money back. We then left and never fucked with him again on no type of business.

I told James and Jason what went down and they couldn't

believe it. They always thought he was a standup guy.

After that day, me and Lil' Mama was together almost every day. I was running a business, hustling hard and playing just as hard. On top of that I had built a bad ass team: Pat, Bedrock, Lucky, Fat Boy, Betty's boyfriend, Junior, my homeboy Jay, my nephews Keith and Javon, Will X, Anita and myself.

Everything was going good. I went out and bought 6 jet skis; the big boys, 5 new cars, a boat and a night club that was used just for the family. Man! We were having a ball. We were rich and living like it. We spent a lot of time on the water. That's where I liked to shine because a lot of ballers didn't know about that type of life. Everything was great. I was thinking that nothing could possibly go wrong, not knowing that half my circle was already plotting. They knew I was getting money and helping them out, but some were plotting nonetheless. They were just going through the motions, just waiting on the opportunity to strike.

Chapter 13

You see Anita didn't hang out with my people too often. She would come through from time to time, but not stay long. She loved the way my family cooked and would come eat, but that was about it. On the other hand I was always around her people. They loved me. So because she didn't come around my people that much, I was able to spend more time with Lil' Mama. We did it all. We played the game. We mostly bullshitted over Betty's house sitting around her big ass pool. After a while, I felt like Barbara was my only woman. We had so much in common. We made love everywhere; even in the pool. She never gave me any problems. Life was good and everything in it.

Although I was now with Barbara, Pat was still in the picture and my family continued to show her love when she came around.

Things were really going well for me at this time. I bought my Lil' Mama another car, and bought my boy Bedrock a truck. It was a 1998 Suburban; it was the biggest truck out on the street at the time. It had an awesome sound system, a television, swivel seats and wooden floors. I also bought him a 2002 Lincoln Navigator which I paid $30,000 cash for. It also came equipped with a nice sound system and televisions as well. I made this purchase for him for one reason; he was my boy, my number one stunner!

I also bought Pat a 1999 Cadillac Seville, which was also equipped with superior sounds and televisions in the dash and head rest. Of course, me and Anita weren't holding them up. We had a

Porsche, a Cadillac, a Navigator, Benzes, Vettes, jet skis and boats. I took care of everybody on the team. Anita and I took care of our own blood families as well. We bought her mother a three hundred thousand dollar house, cars for her Mom and Dad, I bought Jess a car and we looked out for Ann. Anita also looked out for her other sisters as well.

The real estate business was doing great, and we were meeting all the right people. These people were just what we needed to move forward. They included investors, contractors and new title companies. We were doing everything right. I was now also conducting business like a pro. No longer was I just passing out cash while conducting business, or wearing my dickies pants and shirts. I was now wearing the finest suits as well as dealing strictly in checks. Meanwhile, Anita was documenting every transaction for tax purposes and learning how to use Quick Books. She was doing her part and I was doing mine.

I was now coming into the office daily, rolling from the east to the west. Checking on our contractors making sure that everything was going ok and that the contractors were doing what they were supposed to do. Sometimes inspectors would come out and stop the work process on certain properties until we pulled the necessary permits. So, I would go down to the City County building and pull the necessary permits for specific properties and things would go well from there.

I was doing the running for the real estate business, while

simultaneously doing my running for the street business. Everything was on point.

After awhile Anita found out from Pat that I was seeing Barbara. At first she didn't believe it. She had to make sure Pat was telling the truth, so she manipulated Bedrock into telling her just what was going on with Barbara and I. I also slipped up on this one occasion which didn't help the matter. Pat got angry because I had bought this dress for her, but it was too little, so I took it and gave it to Barbara. Well one day Pat had to meet me on Jane to pick up a package and while we were standing in the driveway talking, Barbara came out wearing the dress. I guess she was wearing the shit out of that dress because Pat looked at me like she was about to faint. She asked me if I had given her the dress and I said, yes. I then got smart with her and asked her why should she care. I thought Pat was playing, I didn't really think she cared about that dress like that. But even more, I didn't know that her and Bedrock had completely turned their backs on me and joined ranks with Anita.

Pat couldn't wait to tell Anita what happened. She went and told Anita as soon as she left. Anita was so stunned she actually left the office and came on Jane to see Barbara in this dress. While at the house, Anita was smart and played her role. She asked Barbara for her phone number and said it was for someone else. She then turned around and called her and asked her if we were fucking. Barbara told her that she didn't know what she was talking about. She said that she just rented the house from me and if she wanted to know something like that, she should ask me. At the time, Anita really didn't know for sure that Barbara was my Lil' Mama.

Anita never confronted me or Barbara about Barbara being my girlfriend, but she did tell me that she was kicking Barbara out and that she had to find someplace else to stay. I said okay.

You see my home boy Fat Boy was buying houses, too. He would rent some of his houses out and when he got investors he would sell the other homes to them. So, I asked him could I rent one of his houses out for Barbara and he said yes, he had one available on Faircrest. So I moved Barbara over there.

After that, I figured Anita would get off my back, but I was wrong, that didn't happen. Anita became even more aggressive in this regard. She would start popping up in various locations where I was conducting business. At first I didn't think anything of it. You see Anita knew Pat and I were in a relationship before her and I. So she accepted Pat, but only to a certain point. She also knew she could manipulate Pat because she was weak. Like I said before, Bedrock and Pat were close and talked about everything. Anita also knew that she could talk Bedrock out of whatever she wanted.

Barbara had been living on Faircrest for close to two months before Anita found out where she was. She never caught me over there, but she knew damn well I was going over there. One day however, I think I saw Anita's car on Faircrest. I remember saying, "Damn, that looks like Anita."

How in the hell did she know where Barbara lived this time. At the time, I was puzzled. Never did I think she had gotten the information from Pat and Bedrock. They were telling Anita my every move.

Chapter 14

Anita even went so far as to secure Barbara's phone number from the company's monthly phone records. That's when she approached me about her and accused me of liking her. She said that Barbara was nothing but a hood rat! She then looked at me with disgust and asked me how I could fuck with her when that was my friend Dru's girl. She told me that Barbara had nothing to offer me and then looked at me sideways and asked, "If I was for real." I still denied it. What Anita said to me that day went in one ear and out the other because I didn't care. Barbara and I had everything in common and Anita and I only had our friendship and business. Although I loved Anita very much I wondered if I would have shown Barbara the business what type of life we would have had together.

Man, Barbara and I were making love so much, she got pregnant about six times, but I made her have abortions because I knew Anita was not buying me having no babies on her.

Because business was going so good, Anita wanted me to close down shop and just focus on real estate. I knew if I did that she would have control of all the money. That way, she knew I wouldn't be able to take money and spend it on Barbara, but I went on ahead and quit. I got the team together and told them I was getting out the game. Of course, they weren't really cool with it because everybody liked the fast money and fast life, but I also made them realize that the real estate business was also good money and if we continued like we were going, that everybody could make money and we would never have to look back.

Regardless, Lucky didn't want out. He wanted to stay in the streets, which was cool by me. He was his own man and we were still boys. Or so I thought.

Once I made the move, I really had to get on my J.O.B. I made Bedrock an inspector and Keith got a d.b.a. under the name "Do It Right Construction," Fat Boy opened up his own business, Pat bought houses and Mark worked on them. So now Pat and Mark were doing their own thing like Anita and I, but on a smaller scale. My nephew and his boy were just getting out of jail and they became partners and got a d.b.a. for their construction company.

When my nephew Javon got out of jail it was lovely for him. Everything was set up for him the moment he got out.

My home boy Jay who was the smartest of our team was still locked up during this time, but he knew a lot about the business. So Anita and I would talk to him over the phone asking him different things about the business. Him and Anita talked all the time. Jay helped us set the whole thing up.

As time went on, we were able to buy even more houses. Don't get me wrong, it was not as easy as it sounded, because Anita and I worked hard and I gave up all the money from the streets. Also, we didn't agree on a lot of things. For instance, she didn't want to help my family, but she wanted us to do everything for her family. She also didn't like my nephew and his boy working for us. They were new to the business as I was, but unlike them, I always knew how to manage my money.

There were things I still had to learn though. I knew about running a business as far as the streets went, but I knew little about paying taxes, I didn't like paperwork, nor was I organized when it came to the real estate business, that's why I paid Anita's way through school. That was part of her job.

Nevertheless, I began teaching Keith and Javon all I knew about the business, mainly showing them how to work on houses. I also showed them how to open bank accounts and how to stay on top of their workers. They were young and they were getting a lot of money, the right way. They were also fucking it all up and sometime I had to go behind them to make sure the properties were done right. It was hard to work with them, but they were my nephews and they needed to learn this field. I knew they could show the younger nephews that were coming up how to do it so we could come up as a family.

You see, they were the oldest of the nephews and I figured if I could show them and they turned around and showed the younger nephews, as a family we would be ok. The only problem was they weren't on the same page that I was. They were doing them. The money was coming too fast for them. I had to talk to them every day about different properties they had crews working on and how they had to stay on top of their contractors and workers.

On the other hand, Anita was telling me that I was working too hard. She said that we were paying out tons of money to the contractors and therefore I should let them do the work. She said if they couldn't get it right, fire them and get somebody else. I wasn't cool with that because that would include my two nephews. I needed to get them on track. I can say they were trying, but it was hard because I make everything look so easy. I'm suited and booted every day, but I would work on properties to show Keith and Javon how things were supposed to be done.

Plus, don't forget I had a Lil' Mama I had to hit every day while I was away from the office so I had to get out. Trust me; I knew where Anita was coming from because Keith and Javon were not looking at me as their boss because they didn't know better. I was just Uncle Head to them not Kip. After a while I slowly began to understand what Anita was talking about because we had a lot of people working for us that we had to let go because they were not on our page or couldn't do what we needed them to do. Anita even let her sister Ann go because she wouldn't listen to her.

But, then things got real personal. Anita got to fucking with Keith and Javon's money. I would write them checks and Anita would cancel them. As a result they could only get half of the properties done. They would then complain to me about it. Come to find out Anita was sabotaging them the whole time. The shit was crazy because at first I really didn't know if Anita had cancelled the checks or if they had just jacked the money off. I didn't know who was lying, but wanting to see them through I gave them the rest of the money.

Man, they were off the chain though. They were putting cars in the shop to get painted, were putting all types of sounds and TV's in them and then they would run out of money and have to come to me for more money. I was giving them money and shouldn't have had to, they were getting all types of money; thousands. Nevertheless, I gave them money in spite of their faults and had their backs all the way through like uncles are supposed to do.

More than anything, I just really wanted them to have my back, by going above and beyond as to convince Anita that they were on top of their abilities. I knew if they stayed focused on working and succeeding the right way, they could go very far in the real estate game because I had given and taught them something that no one could take away from them.

Chapter 15

As far as growing our business, Anita was really getting us together. Unlike A&K Investments where we operated like a hood business not paying taxes, etc.: we were really doing business as a legitimate company at First Equity Investments. We had made all the mistakes with A&K, but there was not time for mistakes now. This is how things went.

Anita would find the properties on the internet or through one of our agents who were looking for houses for us. I would then get the property listings and go look at the homes to see if it was worth investing in. I would then determine the condition of the home and any and all damages. Next, I would let Anita know whether or not we could make a sizeable profit from the house. For example, if the house was selling for $20,000, I would determine that it would take $15,000 to rehab. We would give the investor $5,000 and the appraiser three hundred dollars. We would pay the insurance up for a year, which amounted to anywhere between $800 to a $1,000. Then we would do the math.

Our goal was to make a $10,000 profit off each property. We were like Bonnie and Clyde when it came to making money. We were the best team ever. I just wish I would have kept it business and not been in a relationship or whatever it was we were in.

I say this because she was doing her thing while living at the Riverfront and I was living at the River Place doing my thing. We had everything we wanted. She had the key to my apartment and I had the key to her place. That didn't stop me from doing what I was doing, nor did it stop her. There were many times I would go to her place and see boxer shorts that weren't mine. She would tell me they were her sister Ann's boxer shorts, but I knew her sister did not come over that often. I'm no fool.

It wasn't long before I had to move Barbara again because Anita was not lettin' up. See Anita thought I was buying these house for Barbara, not knowing that I was renting them from my home boy Fat Boy. One day I called Fat Boy and said, "Man, I don't know how Anita keeps finding out where Barbara lives, but I got to move her again." I asked him if he had anything for me and he responded that he had a house on Rowe, but it needed some work. I asked him if I could see it. So I looked at it and it did need some work, but it had potential to be a gorgeous place.

The difference between Faircrest and Rowe is Faircrest is in the hood, but Rowe was in a beautiful neighborhood. I showed Barbara the property before I rehabbed it and she liked it then.

The house had a sky roof in the bedroom and I painted the room a real sexy purple which was Barbara's favorite color. I also had marble floors installed throughout the entire house. When I was done having the house rehabbed it was the shit. Barbara was really happy after all the upgrades. I hired this guy named Troy to do the rehabbing, that way Anita wouldn't know about the home's location. At least that's what I thought.

When the house was done Barbara loved it. I placed new

furniture throughout her new abode. I did this all while out of the game. Although I kept a little supply around, I kept just enough to keep a little petty cash on hand. However, I made my money off the contractors.

After a while, Barbara's friends were all beginning to hate on her because she was living good and riding good. They didn't like that at all. They did everything in their power to stop her good fortune. They began to plant seeds in her head by telling her things like I didn't care about her and that she was just a piece of ass to me. Barbara didn't know I had fallen in love with her because like I said, I didn't let her know how much I cared about her.

Looking back, the only people that really cared about me was Pat, even though she was wrong. Fat

Boy, and my home boy Friday did too. Everyone else was just pretending to be my friend. They were great pretenders, but I could see right through them. Pat was on that emotional shit because she knew she had lost me to Anita and now I was seeing Barbara. She thought I wasn't going to be there for her anymore.

Pat and Anita talked about everything. Bedrock didn't really like Anita or Barbara because he felt Anita had taken his place in the food chain and now I was putting another bitch in front of him. Well, I guess him and Pat felt if they told Anita what was going on that would help put an end to Barbara and I, but their plan back fired because Anita used them both to the fullest. Before it was all said and done she would fuck everybody over not just me.

After about four months Anita again found out where Barbara lived. She would ride down the street in different cars stalking me to see if I was over there. Fat Boy used to see her all the time and would tell me, "Man, Anita just rode down the block." On the other hand, even though Barbara was happy about the house, she was sad because I was in and out and she and her son had to move continuously from house to house to keep Anita off our backs. She was having abortion after abortion, but she just loved her Big Daddy. I knew she wasn't happy having abortions and I never meant to hurt her. I just wanted to make her happy, but Anita wasn't having that.

Anita and I spent all our holidays together no matter who we saw on the side. We took trips to spectacular places around the world at least twice a year, or whenever she felt like she wanted me all to herself. One day someone told Anita that I was at Barbara's and what the house looked like. They also told her about the floors, what kind of blinds were up to the windows, what kind of furniture was in the house, the whole nine. Somebody had given her a good description of the entire layout. I knew it couldn't have been Pat because she had never been inside. It also couldn't have been Troy because he never saw the furniture. Only Bedrock knew how the house looked inside, but at the time I couldn't comprehend him telling because he was my main man....my number one stunner.

I knew he probably told Pat how the house looked, but Pat wasn't going to remember details like that.

Anyway to make a long story short, Anita pulled up to Barbara's house, parked the Cadillac on the grass and started screaming, "Kip bring yo ass out of there. Oh you buying bitches houses, that bitch ain't nothing but a hood rat. We're getting money, that bitch is nothing!" Barbara in turn wanted to go out there and beat the brakes off Anita. Be it for the respect she had for Big Daddy, she didn't. I went out, got in my car and Anita and I pulled off.

Man did I hear it that day. All I heard was mothafuckas and how I wasn't shit. Why did I want that bitch while we were making all this money. She shouted how the bitch didn't even have a job and how I had bought her a house, put marble floors in it, blinds, new this and new that. "Bitch," she shouted at me, "You gonna go tear up all that shit and bust them floors up nigga!" I told her I wasn't about to do all that. She responded by telling me that this must mean that you loved that bitch then. My response was, "Ok, whatever Anita get out of my face."

I wasn't stupid I knew after that day that I had to stop seeing Barbara. I had too much to lose on the business side. After that day I didn't go out to Barbara's house for about two or three months. I was giving things a chance to blow over. It didn't matter though because by now, Anita and I were on very bad terms. I would just go to the office, do my job and go home. I still didn't know how in the fuck this bitch knew everything. But, I knew I had to get back cool with her because she was in control of our company which was now worth millions.

The entire time I was away from Barbara I was missing her like crazy. She never knew that I had love for her like that.

Remember, by this time I had only been home from prison for about two years now and as a result, my emotions were all fucked up. I had never really been in a real relationship besides my first love Sonya. When I got out of prison, I got right back to making money and looking for that right one. During this time, I was mad at Sonya because she had gotten married on me and pretty much left me in the hands of my enemies to die. She didn't write me or anything, she just moved on with her life.

Logic would come to me on occasion and I would think about how I left her with a baby who was often sick, no money, no car and no home. I had to come to terms with the fact that she had to do what she had to do to make it out here alone with our child. I should have been happy that the mother of my child was strong like that. Yes, I did the best I could in jail by sending my daughter Toya money, but that was no comparison to what Sonya had to deal with. But, even though like I said, I would think logically about the whole situation from time to time, when I got out of prison my whole thing was to hurt Sonya like she had hurt me. Man was I dumb.

I had come to realize that Pat wasn't the girl for me, nor was Anita. We were just good business partners and that's where it should have stayed. If I had met Barbara before I met Anita and Pat, I know she would have been the one for me.

Sonya had warned me when I came home how the women in

Detroit were, but again I didn't listen. I was still mad at her at the time and I figured she was just hating, but boy would I soon find out exactly what she was talking about.

Chapter 16

After about three months, I finally went back over to Barbara's house on Rowe. When I walked in the front door she was lettin' some nigga out the back. I was in shock. I was pissed. After all I had done for her and she was doing me like this. I was mad as fuck! I never even asked her who the person was, or why she let him out the side door. I didn't care about that. But, I did care about the fact that I was paying all her bills and she had another nigga up in the house. I flipped out! I told her to pack her shit and get the fuck out. She tried to explain to me that it was nothing and how much she loved me, but I wasn't hearing it. I told her to get the fuck out and that I was threw with her. So she packed her shit and headed to her mama's. I was hurt and never even considered what I was taking her through. But, one thing I knew was that, Barbara had now given me a reason. I would never get back on track with Anita until I busted up those floors.

The floors were one thing, but my love for Barbara was another. The love for us was just too strong for me to totally let go. About two days later, I did bust up the floors which made Anita happy. I don't remember if I later got them fixed, but at the time she was happy. I do remember allowing Barbara to go back to the house though.

Barbara was back in the house for about three months when somebody came in on her and robbed her and took my safe. Whoever sent that guy to Barbara's house told him that there was a lot of stuff in the house along with tons of cash. I don't know to this day if

Anita had this done just to make Barbara afraid or what, but Barbara is a fighter. She stabbed the nigga in the shoulder with a big ass knife on his way out the door.

After the robbery, I had to come up with yet another place to move her. I hadn't forgotten about the back door incident though. That really changed me to the point that I knew I had to find me another Lil' Mama for real.

It was about this time that Anita stopped caring about Barbara and I. She was too busy coming up with a plan much bigger than us. She was devising a plan that would ruin me and take everything I owned. As I was preparing Barbara for bigger and better things, Anita was preparing herself for the same. She was opening up different bank accounts and moving money around like the mob.

It was also during this time that for the seventh or eighth time Barbara became pregnant again. This time she refused to have an abortion. Time after time I begged and begged, but she wasn't having it this time. I didn't know what to do except act like I was mad at her, but I wasn't really angry because Lil' Kip, my son, kept coming back. It was like she would go have an abortion, heal up and there was Lil' Kip again, so I accepted that part, but I couldn't let her know. Meanwhile, in my mind, Anita and I were getting' along great. But, of course now because of the baby all that would change.

I knew I would have to tell Anita about the baby. I had to tell her. I figured it was best that she not hear it from someone else…so I told her. She was livid! She responded by telling me that

Barbara was a hoe and because she was a hoe, that she probably wasn't even sure who the baby's daddy was. But, I knew who the daddy was and that was enough for me.

Anita told me that if the baby was mine that she didn't want me to claim it or take care of it because we had worked too hard to get where we were and she gave me an ultimatum: either the child or the money.

Of course I couldn't turn my back on my child. She then told me not to let that bitch get any money out of me for child support. She said if I claimed the baby, she would take every dime I had and that she was not going to take part in taking care of no baby with our money. Real shit.

I thought she was playing. I mean, she had to be crazy. Had she forgotten how she had risen up from nothing just a few years prior, to a multimillionaire all because of our partnership? Was she now about to let this woman on the side dictate the fall of a multimillion dollar empire? I mean she wasn't fucking me, so why should she care that I was fucking somebody else. But, I didn't want to take no chances because she was in control of our cash. And for all intents and purposes, she wasn't about to let the empire fall, she was about to let me fall.

So I took Barbara over to her mother's while she was pregnant so she could lay low. I would sneak over there from time to time to see her, but that was about it. I had to focus most of my attention on Anita.

However, Anita still wasn't fucking, so to satisfy my sex drive I met this lady named Lydia and we became lovers. Lydia had a man and I was doing what I did. It was cool for me this way because Anita was off my back. Lydia and I had a good time whenever we were together. It was not about the love to us, it was just about us having fun and we had plenty of it.

When I first met Lydia, I didn't take her to my apartment in the River Place, I took her to the place on Carrie Street. That's where we talked and got to know each other. That's also where she thought I lived. My nephews Javon and Keith were also there all the time because they would also use the place to bring their women. The house on Carrie was in a pretty good neighborhood. It was a two bedroom, one bath, with a nice living room, dining room and it had nice furniture. Lydia liked it.

Lydia was a fine yellow bone, strapped from head to toe, thick as hell and smart as a whip. She knew what she wanted out of life. She was working at this phone place called Page Tel up on Gratiot when I met her. Her bosses' name was Ray, he was cool. Lydia ran the place and soon actually bought the place from him. She was going to school and all that good stuff. She just liked to have fun. She, her sister and her friends would hit the town and they really knew how to party. Lydia worked hard and played hard. She was my type of girl and we got along just great.

I think we got along so great because we didn't have any ties. She didn't have to answer to me and I didn't have to answer to her. I called her Niece Niece and she called me Unk Unk. I didn't party with them because that was not my type of hype. I'm old school and I don't like clubbing unless I own the club, otherwise I don't club like that. My nephews were representing me well, they were out there getting' it in!

After a short while I showed Lydia where I lived because she was so cool. Man, when I first took her to my apartment I had no furniture, no beds or nothing. I had given it all away, but the new stuff was coming the next day. But, even without the furniture, when she saw the place she went crazy. It was the first time she had ever seen anything like it.

That night we made love all through my penthouse. On the floor, on the kitchen counter top, the steps, everywhere. We were like two wild rabbits on the loose. She was my nigga and just as wild as me.

At this time Anita and I had the business running off the chain. It could only get better. Anita knew I was not fucking Barbara anymore, so in my mind we were cool. Not so much just because I wasn't fucking Barbara, but because I was also out of the streets and working harder on my end of the business.

In reality however, Anita had plotted that by the time she took everything, that I wouldn't have anything, because I had let all my plugs go. Anita played her role and kept her anger about Barbara and her pregnancy under control.

The furniture arrived the next day and my penthouse was back on point. I topped everything off with a few arcade games worth five thousand dollars; a Ms. Pac Man, a Centipede and a Defender game. Also arriving was my bar and a weight set. A total of $15,000 in merchandise. It was off the chain. Everybody who came over loved it.

Chapter 17

When the team wasn't working, we were on the water having a ball with the boats and jet skis. All the while Anita was keeping my agenda on point. I was having at least one contractor's meeting a month. At the contractor's meetings we would talk about what we expected of them. We would let them know that if we lost money because of them not keeping up their end of the contracts, we would deduct money from them every day they went over the set completion date.

Our company was getting bigger and bigger by the day. We had an additional 15 contractors that we were feeding, not including the additional staff in the office. Man we had some good contractors and they loved us for what we were doing for them.

With the amount of houses we were buying each month, we were making out like bandits. We had good appraisers who gave us good comps, which we needed. We had some other good people like Leonard and James; they helped us find good houses for the low-low in good neighborhoods. We had good title companies and we created our own market.

To celebrate our good fortunes, we had our first company picnic. We invited everybody; the investors, the contractors and everybody in the office. It took place at Metro Beach. It was wonderful; we had all kinds of food, drinks and music. And of course we brought the jet skis. It was the best company picnic ever. Anita and I were like two in one. We played our role to the tee and let everyone know we really appreciated them to the fullest. We were like the character in the movie Scarface; we wanted the world Chico and everything in it.

One day, Friday, our housing inspector and I were out in the field checking on some properties for potential purchase when Anita called all upset saying Barbara kept calling her phone fucking with her. I didn't believe it was Barbara playing on the phone though. I knew better. If anything, Anita was doing the playing on the phone, but I heard her out. Then I told her I knew she had been fucking with Barbara all month and had even offered her $6,000 to get rid of our baby. I also informed her that I knew she had told Barbara that I was fucking other women and that she was stupid for fucking with me. She even went on to tell me that she told Barbara that I was also fucking Lydia. When she said that I got to wondering how in the hell did she know about Lydia? As I was talking to Anita I was pulling up to my office with Friday.   I went upstairs, walked into the office and shut the door to Anita's office. I then asked her why was she fucking with that girl and that's when she went crazy. She picked up a chair and cracked me upside the head with it. Friday was in the office watching this with amazement. After she hit me upside the head with the chair I was mad as hell, so to keep my anger under control, I stepped out of the office to grab my bearings and she locked the door behind me with Friday still in the office while she called the police. She told Friday to say that I had hit her when the police came but he refused to lie. He said that he wouldn't and that I was his friend. As a result she fired him. When the police got there they asked what happened and I told them that she had hit me in the head with a chair. Of course she denied it and told them that she was the sole owner of the business and showed them the corporation papers. That's when I found out my name as a partner had been whited out. As a result, the police escorted me out of the building.

Almost until the very end, I really did love Anita, but I was not in love with her. She was more like a best friend and good business partner. After the police walked me out of the building, she called me and we met up. She said she had told the police what she told them so I wouldn't get out of control. I told her it was already out of control because she had hit me with a chair. She responded that I deserved what I got for taking up for that hood rat bitch. I told her that I wasn't taking up for her, but okay cool, whatever. Remember, I hadn't really seen Barbara at all. She had called me and told me what Anita was saying, but I was not going to disclose this to Anita. Anita and I were doing so good with the business, that I didn't want to ruffle any feathers. I was trying to stay away from Barbara so Anita wouldn't get control of my money; well at least my half, but little did I know it was too late.

I told her that because she thought she was in control of the money that she could just play me any kind of way. I told her that we could just split the money and I could just be on my way. That's when she told me she couldn't do that because she didn't have all of her I's dotted and T's crossed so she wasn't prepared to split up the money at that time.

I would later come to learn, that Anita had already been sending money overseas and hiding money from me everywhere. She had used the baby as an excuse, but the truth is Anita was robbing me from day one.

Chapter 18

After that day, whenever I would ask Anita about the books, she would give me the run around. She would start talking about something else, delaying giving me an answer. After about a month or so she again took me for a loop and had me thinking everything was cool. She set up a trip telling me that we needed a break. That we had been working too hard and needed to go somewhere to relax. So she set up a trip to Cancun and off we went. We stayed for four or five days and had a ball. We fucked and everything. Well her plan worked. That stopped me from asking about the books and things again were going great.

While we were gone, I left my nephew the keys to my penthouse, the Benz, the Cadillac as well as access to the boat and jet skis. They had a ball. This was during the time there was a blackout in Detroit. I was told it was hot as hell and niggas was sitting on their porches with shot guns. People had to charge their phones up in the car, the city was out of gas and there was no ice. Javon was somewhat good because he was at my penthouse where we had a working generator that came on as soon as the blackout hit. It was crazy. Nobody could be trusted. I was in the pool drinking Margaritas when my nephew Javon called and told me what was going on. I couldn't believe it. I told Anita and we both checked on our families to make sure everyone was okay. Anita and I missed all of that.

When we returned to Detroit everything was back to normal. Anita told me that I needed to know her end of the business and she needed to know mine. However, instead of Anita showing me her end, she was adamant that she go out in the field first to see how my end operated. It was a mess, but well planned out.

Contractors immediately started complaining. Anita would ask them all types of questions while they were trying to work and they didn't like that at first. With the knowledge I had given her and with her questioning them, soon she became a pro about my end of the business. When I tried to learn her end, she would just show me bits and pieces and never allow me to formulate a full picture. Little did she know I was already up on her game, I just didn't want her to know I knew what she was doing. Anita thought I was a dumb ass, but I guess you can say I was in a sense because of the love I possessed for our friendship. As she became more comfortable with the contractors and they became more comfortable with her, she started putting her plan into action because time was running out.

She started telling the contractors that I beat her every day, that I treated her like shit and that I had another woman. She told them that I wouldn't allow her to do anything, go anywhere and therefore she was going to close the business and that they could make a whole lot more money fucking with only her. She told them that First Equity was going to close in about 8 months.

The contractors believed her, not realizing they should have asked themselves one question; when had Anita ever missed a day off work besides when the two of us were out of town? How and when could I have allegedly beaten her? Anita doesn't wear too much makeup, so where were the bruises? She played the victim role to all of my employees to a tee. She told them she was going to give me half of the money and all that good shit.

Anita's plan was going well and was well thought out. You see, this is a dirty bitch that cares about nothing but money because her plan was to rob me, disappear and probably have me killed. If that didn't work, one way or the other her goal was to have me locked up for the rest of my life. At this point who would believe me if I tried to speak out? She had a master plan. She was a law abiding citizen with no criminal background who had a Master's Degree in Business who helped out the community, not to mention she was a church going woman. Whereas, I had a criminal record, so it would be all over for me.

During this time my lease was up at the River Place and they would not renew it because they said I was coming in and out with too many different cars and women. They thought I was selling drugs, but of course I wasn't. There was no need to…the business was at an all-time high. Thinking back, I was never late on a payment, nor did I give management any problems, I always did whatever they asked. It had to be Anita once again dishing dirt.

Nevertheless, I knew where ever I moved next, I had to top the River Place and that would not be easy.

My home boy Tiger told me about some places in Troy that were very nice. He took me to look at some of these places and they were all right. When we got to the last place on the list, Regent Park, Man! When we pulled into the complex it was nice, I liked it, but that was only the beginning. The penthouse was out cold; 3,600 square feet of pure luxury. I had to have it.

The people in the rental office didn't give me any problems. I showed them all of my papers and I was good to go. My new address was 2659 Melcombe, Apt. 402.

I told Anita that I had found another penthouse and she acted like she liked it. I again went looking for furniture so that I could do what I had done at the River Place. I gave away all my old stuff except the video games. I was on top of the world! I bought a cream colored dining room table with the matching colored chairs, a cream white bar with gold trim around it, pink and cream furniture with two tower stands about 6 feet tall and to top it off, I bought some pink and cream flowers and placed them on top of the stands. I also had a real fire place with two white ceramic pots on each side.

In each bedroom I had a big ass king sized bed with matching dressers. I didn't stop there; the entire bathroom was pink, cream and white.

My bar was the shit: Order up! I had every kind of liquor you could imagine.

Anita's Dad used to come see me all the time and I had informed the office that my Dad was deaf and was allowed to visit even when I wasn't home. You see Mr. Power and I were cool like that. He used to come and get money and weed from me whenever Anita wouldn't give it to him. We had a good relationship. He was a man who really loved his girls. He also loved the race track. He used to tell me that he was gonna hit big one day.

Even though I already had numerous luxury cars, I couldn't get a new apartment without doing it up big in the form of transportation, so I put a down payment on a Bentley!

Anita and I went and put a $5,000 down payment on the Bentley. I don't know why we just didn't pay it off then, of course now I do, but I should have just paid for it outright. She rationalized not paying for it out right by telling me that we needed to save that money and get a house instead. So we started looking for a mansion.

She said we were paying too much for our apartments as it was, so I said, okay. As a result, I called my man James and told him that I was looking for a house somewhere close to my penthouse.

Around the corner from me was Jack Christianson's office. He was the real estate broker that James worked for. I let him know that I was staying right around the corner not knowing that Anita had already made him abreast of our situation and told him to watch out for me. James came over and we talked for a while concerning him looking for me a new house.

Rasheed Wallace, a member of the Detroit Pistons, moved into the vacant penthouse next to mine. He was always aloof and barely ever spoke, but when I found out who he was, I have to admit it was kind of exciting having someone of his stature living next door.

James was elated about Rasheed living there because he figured if he could get his attention long enough, maybe he could find him a house and get a big commission. So he slid his business card under his door and waited for the call.

I don't know if he ever received his big call, but James did find my dream home. It was gorgeous. It even had a 12 foot lighted swimming pool in the lower level. I had to have it. I told Anita about it and we put down $8,000 in good faith money to get the ball rolling.

I never did get the house though because James came back to the table saying that there was a problem and blah, blah, blah.

James was my friend so I can't imagine what Anita might

have said to turn him against me, but then again the contractors were also my friends. I guess whatever money she offered was worth more than our friendship. Most of these men had families to feed and they weren't use to the kind of money they were making and they sure weren't about to take a chance and lose it by crossing Anita.

Whatever she told James about her plans concerning what she was about to do with our business, it must have impacted him enough to believe I was going to be left with nothing. Bear in mind that he was number one in monthly commissions at Jack Christian's realty since he had known Anita and I. So he was not about to let that go by messing with Kip. Knowing Anita was shuffling and dealing the cards.

After that, Anita and I met with the C.P.A. and our lawyer who counseled us on how to secure more bank accounts. In actuality, she was also bringing them into her fold. Just introducing me so they could see who I was. In reality I would later find out that she had already put them up on what was going on a year earlier.

When we later started having court battles, I wondered why she had the business moved to an address in Oakland County. Well come to find out, it was something that her lawyer had advised, knowing it would be better for him in Oakland County versus Detroit where he had no relations with Detroit judges. That way when everything went down, I would have to face an Oakland County judge. A two-time felon vs. a stellar young college millionaire graduate.

All of this was really a shame, because after all, I didn't give Anita all my energy to fuck over me. I gave it to her so we could help others as well as ourselves.

Chapter 19

I must say that Anita was on her job. Back at the office, everyone knew what was going on except me.

It wasn't long before Anita started bad mouthing the contractors saying that they weren't doing what they were supposed to do and were talking back to her. She started saying how we had to go hard and start firing people. She said the investors weren't happy. So I started back checking on the contractors. I was now on them harder than ever telling them that things weren't right and how things had to be done. I told them that if they couldn't do it right, then I would find someone else to do it. Meanwhile, they were looking at me like I was crazy as hell, saying to themselves, maybe Kip does have her afraid. She now had me and the team twisted.

We ended up firing most of the contractors except for Keith, Javon, Roy Power, Jay, Mars, Andy and two others. I was cool that she didn't fire my nephews, but I was fucked up. I just couldn't seem to get a handle on which direction she was going in.

While I was out fucking up my reputation and helping to fire our current team, Anita was out creating a whole new team.

One day I came in the office and she told me with tear filled eyes that she had checked on the houses and somebody had vandalized 10 of them and that we didn't have the money in the budget to fix them back up. Sure as heck, when I went out and checked, the houses were destroyed. Seeing her cry didn't make things easier. I was a sucker for love. I called my homeboy Carl who had a reputation for rehabbing houses within 30 days and we went into action. We had all the houses back in tip top shape in enough time to continue making money off of them.

I later found out that Anita had one of our contractors vandalize the properties so as to throw me off while she did what she had to do. I was out of the office from 7 a.m. to 9 p.m. sometimes until 10:00 at night.

To continue to throw me off, she told me how proud she was that I had rehabbed all the ruined houses and as a treat she had purchased more tickets to Cancun. Fixing those houses had taken a physical toll on me, so a trip to Cancun was right on time.

Keep in mind, I was happy during this time because most of what I'm writing about now, I didn't find out until much later during court depositions. I was also happy because my son had been born giving me a reason to be even more elated.

Regardless of how she felt about my child, I was not about to turn my back on Lil' Kip.

The first time I found out that Anita was manipulating bank accounts happened one day when I went to pay rent. Yes, she was that busy setting things up that she forgot to pay the rent. You see Anita used to pay all my bills and everything. I simply gave her too much control over my life. After filling out the bank slip for $3,000 the teller asked me which account I wanted the money to come out of. I was stunned, I started wondering what she was talking about, but then she asked me again which account. She asked if I wanted it to come out of the Home Funding. I'm thinking maybe she was saying the name wrong so I said, yes. Then she said I couldn't get money out of that account because my name wasn't on it. I almost passed out believing Anita had created the account intentionally.

I quickly gathered myself and called Anita and asked her about this Home Funding account. Anita was slick and kept her cool. She said that it had slipped her mind to tell me, but she and the accountant had made some changes and for me not to worry, she was on her way to the bank to add my name to the account.

I was upset, but I calmed down a bit knowing she was on her way.

Shortly thereafter, Anita arrived and put my name on the account. I guess she thought she wasn't going to hear anything else from me about it, but she was wrong. Now I really wanted to see the books, which I still hadn't seen. I asked her where the books were and she simply said she would show them to me, but she kept stalling. I guess she had more changes to make before she showed them to me.

Also, I'm sure she had to tell her family what was going on just in case things went bad. I'm sure that's just what they wanted to hear though, that Anita and I weren't getting along and therefore she was going to have to do what she had to do. I later found out she told them that we only had $366,000 in the First Equity account and that we were going to split that. Which was true. But there was a lot more money involved here. They didn't know "jack shit!" There was far greater than six million dollars involved that she had taken and put into different accounts that she had created. We made three million dollars our first year alone in business.

Meanwhile, I was still working on the houses. I think I was driving the Navigator at the time, which was in her mother or father's name, the Porsche we supposedly sold to my home boy. My friend Chester was leasing the Cadillac truck from Anita and I and Anita was driving the Benz.

Well she told me the Benz needed to go in the shop and that she was going to get a rental. I always let her drive the best cars, so I gave her the Navigator and took the rental. Now at this point, I had a rental car, my phone and an American Express card. Dig how she figured out how to get the phone from me.

She asked me to go to the mall with her then asked if she could use my phone. I was tired as hell from working on the houses and wasn't paying attention, but she never gave me my phone back. When I asked her for it she said she lost it. She had me and her sister looking all over the mall for my phone. After we couldn't find it she told me not to worry about it, we would go the following day and get another one. I told her that was cool, then I brought back up the books.

This time she said okay, she would show them to me. So we went and dropped Jazz off, then she dropped me off at my place. After I got to my place I jumped in the rental and headed to her apartment. When I got there I let myself in. As I opened the door to her apartment, I heard her on the phone with some guy. I told her to get off the phone and show me the books and she replied, "I'm not showing you the books Kip."

I asked her why every time I asked her about the books it was the same ole story, but she tried to divert things by acting like her phone conversation was more important than what I was talking about. So again, I told her to let me see the books and again she tried to occupy the phone.

But, this time I wouldn't let her. I was getting angrier by the minute. I went into the kitchen and got a box of drinking glasses that were sitting on the counter and took the entire box back to the den where she was now sitting. I began to remove one glass at a time and began tossing them against the wall right over her head. I told her that I had no intentions of hurting her. I just wanted to see the books.

This time she yelled, "No." So, I threw another glass at the wall while yelling, "I said turn over the books!" This time the glass shattered and a piece of glass cut into her leg. It cut her to the point where she would need stitches.

The minute I saw the blood, I became more concerned about her leg than the books. As she began to cry, I started feeling sorry for her. I ran and got a big towel from the bathroom and wrapped her leg to stop the bleeding. I then began apologizing to her and letting her know how sorry I was. I was a mess.

She put on her sweet caring voice and told me not to worry, that she knew I didn't mean it and everything would be okay. She suggested we call Jay, my home boy that Anita had maintained a relationship with the entire time he was incarcerated. By this time he was both of our friend and would often act as a go between when we would have problems. When we were alone though, he used to tell me that I was a better man than him because Anita was robbing me blind.

When he arrived he talked to us and advised us that we both had too much to lose. He asked Anita if she wanted us or him to take her to the hospital and she said, "No that I was a good man and she didn't want any trouble."

Now I've forgotten all about the books because my concern now was about her, (my emotions were all fucked up). This couldn't have happened any better for her in helping her with her plan.

Anita said that she wasn't mad at me, but the wound was too deep, she had to go to the hospital for stitches. She told us that we didn't need to go, that she would drive herself there, so she left and went to the hospital while me and my boy stayed at the apartment for about 35 more minutes talking.

Before she left, Anita said she would call me and let me know that she was alright. She called later that evening on my house phone and said she was okay and that she had stitches, but she was alright and was gonna spend the night at her Mom's house.

The following day she called and asked me to meet her at her mother's. She knew that I was feeling terrible about the cut. When I arrived at the house she was sitting across the couch with her legs crossed with a blue bandage wrapped around her injured leg. She had told her mother and other family members that she had run into her glass table. At least that's the story she told me she told them. Anyway, I stayed and kicked it for a while. We watched television, talked and ordered something to eat. I hoped that talking would make her feel better.

What I didn't know is while she and I were together, her team was moving all her things out of the office and to her new office in Southfield. She had changed the name of the new company to Visions. The only thing she left at the old office was a computer and a desk. She took all of my office furniture and stored it in a storage facility across the street from the 36th District Court. I think she used that storage area just in case if things went bad she would be close to authorities. She even deleted all of my files.

Anyway, when I got ready to leave, Anita reminded me that we were going to Cancun in a couple of days to work out our problems and that everything would be okay. She also said that she was going to take me to get my new phone the following day. Just buttering me up for the kill. Lastly, she told me that the new account that I signed my name to was our savings account, so not to worry because everything was cool in that regard. So I said okay. After all we were headed to Cancun.

Chapter 20

The very next day, for all intents and purposes, I was broke. This was May 2004.

Anita called and said she was on her way to pick me up, but never made it. Instead, she went over to my Aunt's house where she left a box filled with paper, along with a breakdown of some $134,000 which was my half of the money. Now to the average person that was a lot of money, but to me, that was nothing compared to the millions that I knew she was hiding.

She had my Aunt call and tell me that I could go to the bank and get my half of the money and that she and I was through. I was fucked up. I didn't know what to do.

I picked up the house phone to call Anita and her phone was disconnected. I then started calling the contractors and they were all acting as though they didn't know what was going on. I called Roy and he said that he didn't know what was going on either and that he wasn't trying to get caught up in our problems.

When I went to the office everything was gone. The place was empty. Of course I was fucked up. I then went to Anita's Mom's in a rage. I figured Anita was there, but her Mom didn't want to hear anything I had to say because as far as she was concerned, I'd gotten my half of the money so what could be the problem.

Remember she's deaf, so she wrote something on a piece of paper which read, "You always asked her to split the business." I responded,

"No, she robbed me!" I kicked the little table over and was about to go out the door until I heard Jess talking to Anita on the phone. Not thinking, I tried to tussle the phone away from her, but gave up after I saw she wasn't trying to give me the phone.

The next thing I knew, I was a fugitive. The police were looking for me for aggravated assault relative to the glass throwing incident that happened months earlier. Anita had pressed charges on me and told them that I cut her in the leg with a knife and she was afraid for her life.

When they finally caught up with me, it was crazy. I couldn't believe it. In order to avoid prison I had to plead to a lesser charge because they were gonna charge me with two counts of assault with a dangerous weapon and a 4th degree habitual offender charge and with my record, that meant the possibility of life in prison. Wow! So in addition to breaking me financially this bitch succeeded in sending me to prison. I ended up receiving 18 months' probation and 6 months in the Dickerson Correctional Facility with work release and 45 days on a tether.

So, in addition to breaking me financially, this bitch done sent me to jail! What the fuck!

Before I was sentenced, her family put personal protection orders against me because I had kicked the table over and tried to take the phone out of Jess's hand. Anita had a protection order in Pontiac and Detroit which read as follows: Any and all documents, financial reports, notes of any kind or nature in your possession or control concerning any type of financial matter for Home Brokers Funding of Michigan, Inc., First Equity Investment Corporation and Anita Power personally must be returned to her at once, because I had gone to the Riverfront Apartments and got her mail. I also went to the Penobscot Building and picked up our mail there to try and find out what was going on.

I remembered that I had a list for the upcoming properties, so I took a ride and guess who I ran into? Roy! Sneaking and working on one of the properties. I then ran into Andy working on another property. As I drove by all the other homes, I see all our contractors working on the properties. Now I'm asking myself what is going on because I knew these were all First Equity properties, but I knew I had to keep my anger under wraps. I wanted to express to all of them how I was feeling though, without making things any worse.

I told the contractors that Anita had robbed me and that they must cease and desist any and all work on all of the properties. I think at the time God took over, because Anita had used her anger in a negative way to get what she wanted and I didn't want to go that far with the contractors. I wanted to leave the door open for future communication so I pretty much told them that they had to stop working on the houses, but I didn't get violent about it.

Anita had become so manipulative, that I believe she had even started to believe her own hype. She got her way for the time being, but in the long run I was sure her deceitful ways would catch up with her. She had humiliated me in front of everybody: the staff, both our families, the contractors, our friends, everybody. While using our money to control everybody in the process.

One by one each contractor started calling Anita telling her that I was showing up at the work sites asking questions. My goal was not to intimidate them, I just wanted them to know at this point that I knew what was going on, however, that I was not going to be pushed around. But, deep inside I was threw. Although my anger was at an all-time high and I felt like a jerk, I felt powerless and hopeless.

I had received personal protection orders from Jess Power, Anita Power and one from Ann Power, who informed me that the only reason she sought and obtained the order was because Anita told her to.

I responded to all their motions for the personal protection orders and asked the court to conduct a hearing for the protective orders to explain why I wanted the orders modified or terminated. The protective orders were based on false swearing and false allegations; because when I kicked the table and tried to take the phone I never meant to hurt anyone.

It was Anita that embezzled money from our business, had me falsely arrested and had all of these fraudulent protective orders filed against me. She filed the PPO as a pre-emptive action before the discovery of the theft of my money.

The Oakland County judge wasn't trying to hear anything from my lawyer or myself. Once, while I was standing facing the judge, Anita's father came up behind me and punched me in the back of the head hard as hell. Angry, he was under the assumption that Anita had given me my half of the proceeds to dissolve our business relationship. That I was beating on his daughter every day. Like I had betrayed his trust in our friendship. That was very untrue. He knew only what Anita told him which was a pack of lies. She did not tell him that she had transferred a million or more dollars out of First Equity bank accounts. Or that she purchased 80 homes that came out of First Equity accounts and put them in a company name that was unknown to me at the time. In addition she still had two million dollars in a trust account that I wasn't supposed to know about. But her cousin Bow told me. Which is the reason why she placed the PPO against me and lied to her father and others about my behavior to put me in jail to keep me from the portion of my money. And the fact that she did not want me to take care of my new born child. It took four or five offices to restrain him. Finally they got him down to the floor and put him out of the court room. The judge kept asking me did I want to press charges against him, but I couldn't bring myself to do it because all he knew was what Anita had told him.

In the meantime, Anita told the contractors to go ahead and stop working for the time being because I would be locked up shortly, so not to worry. She was doing everything in her power that I not only go to jail, but I get an additional sentence for not following the protective orders.

After I went to jail, she had two more properties vandalized and told the court that while I was supposed to be out on work release, that I had vandalized the properties. Little did she know, when I was sent to Dickerson, I just did the time. I never did my work release, I just did the time so that plan didn't work.

You see I knew Anita was a snake in the grass and that if I was on the streets she would conjure up something else. She thought I would be out from 7 a.m. to 6 p.m. Well this time the trick was on her because I didn't leave the facility at all, I stayed there 24 hours. Anita told the court that I was following her and playing on her phone; she didn't know that I had chosen jail over dealing with her.

It was by far the smartest and safest move I had made thus far.

Chapter 21

I ended up only doing 45 days in Dickerson. I had to go home with a tether box on my leg and do 18 months' probation. Here's the thing. Remember I was still living next door to Rasheed Wallace so it was a good thing that I never had to run into him while my tether was going off at 3:00 in the morning. Whenever it would go off I would have to go outside and walk my tether like a dog to prove I was home.

That would have been embarrassing.

Wow, it's funny now, but back then I would go outside and think to myself you have got to be kidding me. I had to laugh to keep from going crazy because this bitch had pulled off the perfect storm.

After I got out of jail and got my thoughts together, I decided to play her game and fight her in the courts. So I went into action. I hired Sam Gun and his buddy Arnold Sword to take my case. Believe it or not, no other lawyers would take my case saying things like the case was like a bad divorce and they didn't want any parts of it.

Once Anita realized she couldn't get me booked by lying on me in the city of Detroit, she started her mess up again in Pontiac. The officials in Pontiac didn't know what was going on. Anita told them I called her phone and threatened her and once again I was back in court for violating my probation.

It was frustrating because they thought I was crazy. They ordered me to obtain outpatient substance abuse and mental health counseling with another curfew letter to be in by 7:00 p.m.

Once a week I had to go see a psychiatrist named Mr. Bruno. Every time I saw him I had to pay a hundred and twenty five dollars per session. I explained to Mr. Bruno what was going on and he believed me. He knew that I wasn't crazy and put in a request to the court to talk to Anita, but he never got to see her. The good thing at this point was that I was not in jail, but she continued to try and get me locked up.

After a short period of time, I went into action and my attorney contacted her attorney with a lawsuit. What Anita didn't know was that I had learned how to handle my anger in more productive ways when I was locked up for those 10 years. I had learned to manage patience so that it would be a benefit to me when I got out, not a liability. During this time that training kicked in because I was going through situation after situation that I could neither control or change.

Ironically, I was assigned an officer of the court named Brandy Stitts, who desperately tried to show the court that not only was I no kin to her, but that I violated my protection order.

During this time I was overwhelmed. I was trying to take care of my family and other responsibilities. I was still trying to open and run a new business while also paying lawyers to take Anita to court. It was really hard because she had left me with just enough to fight her in court. I kept asking myself who I was the most angry with, Anita or myself. For the life of me I couldn't figure out which.

When Anita's protective order against me expired, she tried to renew it. I asked the judge for a hearing and stated that Anita was a calculated, egotistical, and self-centered, conniving, hot mess. Again, this was Oakland County and the judge didn't want to hear it. Knowing this, Anita continued playing her role before the judge. She said she was very afraid of me and acted as if I was gonna kill her. She was something else. She would arrive to court 15 minutes late with two huge body guards wearing black suits looking like security for Lil' Kim.

After getting a subpoena and receiving some of the bank statements, I couldn't believe what Anita had done. She had written out huge checks and taken out substantial loans in my name. I had no idea what else she had done. I hate to imagine.

In the meantime, she was back on track. The original contractors were back working on the houses, but after Anita realized she didn't need them anymore, she got rid of them all and got her own. She fucked over a whole group of people, their families and friends without one bit of remorse.

I can't believe we went to church together every Sunday; donating money, the whole nine. She had those church people fooled.

Chapter 22

During the court depositions
of my lawsuit against Anita, which
she took as a game, whenever Anita
would turn over paper work, I knew
I had to pay close attention, because
I knew what Anita was capable of
and how creative she was. The
more I looked at the books, the
easier it was for me to understand
how she had moved the money.
How she pretended she put money
in one account, but didn't at all.

I knew she made up the bank
statements because hers didn't
match what I received back from
the subpoenas. I told the lawyers
that all the records were made up,
but the judge didn't want to hear it,
saying that going further into the
correct records would open up
another whole can of worms....like

he had something else to do other than preside over my case.

In spite of everything I was going through, I knew God had my back. I knew he wouldn't put any more on me than I could take. I believed that.

Funny thing, I recently came across this poem by Mary Oliver which reads:

Someone that I loved gave me a box full of darkness,

It took me years to understand that this too, was a gift.

It was nowhere near the amount of money I lost, but the court awarded me $80,000. Anita was ordered to pay me $5,000 a month until the amount was reached.

Now I understand, a lesson well learned. That box of darkness that I received was a gift.

TO BE CONTINUED

Coming Soon

(Double the Trouble)

After all I had been through with Anita, I never thought that I would go through it ever again. I thought I had learned a valuable lesson and that no woman would ever be able to get over or take me through it again. Little did I know that not only would I go through it again, but I would go through it with double the trouble.

To some people, they saw me as being vulnerable or just weak because Anita did not come up dead or hurt. What they didn't know was Anita had all her (T's) crossed and (I's) dotted and if any and I mean anything happened to her she had set everything up which would have made it look like Kip did it.

So, I made myself unassailable because I could have gotten locked up for life. I prayed every day that Anita stayed safe because the police would have come to me first. So in spite of all the storms and situations, I just fell back because I was no fool.

The Perfect Storm

39433067R00106

Made in the USA
Lexington, KY
23 February 2015